INSIGNIA OF THE WAFFEN-SS

Hofphotograph
SAARBRÜCKEN

Insignia of the Waffen-SS

Cuff Titles • Collar Tabs
Shoulder Boards • Badges

ROLF MICHAELIS

4880 Lower Valley Road • Atglen, PA 19310

Originally published as *Die uniformspezifischen Abzeichen der Waffen-SS*,
© 2010 by Rolf Michaelis, Berlin, Germany.
Translated from the German by David Johnston.

Library of Congress Control Number: 2016942470

Cover design by Matthew Goodman
Type set in Minion Pro/Times New Roman
ISBN: 978-0-7643-5176-1
Printed in China
5 4 3 2

Published by Schiffer Publishing, Ltd.
4880 Lower Valley Road
Atglen, PA 19310
Phone: (610) 593-1777; Fax: (610) 593-2002
E-mail: Info@schifferbooks.com
Web: www.schifferbooks.com

Other Schiffer Books by the Author:
Assault Badges of the Wehrmacht in World War II (978-0-7643-4257-8)
Close Combat Badges of the Wehrmacht in World War II (978-0-7643-4258-5)
German Wound Badges in World War II (978-0-7643-4259-2)
The Third Reich Bravery and Merit Decoration for Eastern Peoples (978-0-7643-4803-7)
The German Tank Destruction Badge in World War II (978-0-7643-4052-9)
The German Anti-Partisan Badge in World War II (978-0-7643-4260-8)

CONTENTS

PREFACE

Rolf Michaelis specializes in books on the Waffen-SS and has written over thirty to date, with many available in English from Schiffer Books. He lives in Berlin.

In 2001, I published the book *Die Waffen-SS: Uniformen und Abzeichen*, where the main emphasis was on the field of uniforms. Since then I have placed more focus on the field of badges, and this has reached a degree of completeness that makes a publication of its own seem to make sense.

I was aided in this by the fact that over the past twenty-two years I have archived experience reports by former members of the *Waffen-SS* as well as photographic material. Not only was I able to analyze the veterans' wartime photos, but photos of their various mementoes as well. I also received support from those with an historical interest, who kindly made their collections available to me. I would like to thank them all, especially Robert Fabisiak, Leo Tammiksaar, and Hans Wikke.

This book documents the history of the *Waffen-SS* from a very special perspective. The possibility of conveying previously unknown information and perhaps providing food for thought almost exclusively through images seemed especially interesting to me. Surely, more than a few readers will shake their heads and say that it is hard to believe that, for example, even Armenians served in the *Waffen-SS*!

Those who wish to learn more about the *Waffen-SS* are advised to seek out my many other publications concerning its formation and operational history.

Using nearly 300 color images of collar patches, shoulder straps, sleeve badges and cuff titles, this book reveals the scope that the *Waffen-SS* achieved by the end of the war and how far it strayed from Himmler's original principles because of the steadily deteriorating military situation. It merely touches on the many manufacturing variants, however, and cannot tackle the problem of identifying original versus reproduced badges. The *Waffen-SS* predecessor—the *SS-Verfügungstruppe*—the *SS-Totenkopfverbände*, and *Allgemeine-SS* are only touched on only briefly.

Unfortunately, it also cannot show the suffering that the Second World War brought to the people. The reader may bear in mind the millions of individual fates—especially as the time that separates us from them grows ever greater.

Rolf Michaelis
Berlin, August 2009

INTRODUCTION

As in other European states in the 1930s and 1940s, uniforms also played a special role in the Third Reich. Unity and equality prevailed in the numerous state organizations and this allowed the German people to be divided optically into specifically uniformed groups—alongside the diminishing number of civilians. In addition to the approximately sixteen million members of the *Wehrmacht* (army, air force and navy), these included the SA, the *Reichskriegerbund* (War Veterans Association), the *Reichsarbeitsdienst* (Reich Labor Service), the *Hitlerjugend* (Hitler Youth), the *Organisation Todt*, the police, the German Red Cross, the *Reichsbahn* (State Railroad) and the *Waffen-SS*.

Within each of these organizations there were differences for special services or branches or designations of rank. In the *Waffen-SS* in particular, with about a million members from thirty countries, there was an especially wide variety of uniform-specific insignia. While the uniform itself underwent few changes during the war years, over time a total of more than 140 different collar tabs, rank and activity badges, sleeve shields (also often called nationality shields) and cuff titles were introduced. As well, there were about twenty different branch-of-service colors for the individual branches.

In 1935, the *Leibstandarte der SS "Adolf Hitler"* became the first armed formation of the SS, receiving an earth-grey uniform and with it new badges. An eagle worn on the sleeve, which was not yet present on the black uniform of the *Allgemeine-SS*, was introduced, and the cap eagle and Death's Head emblem were modified. As well, a second shoulder strap was worn, which as of 1938, reflected the wearer's rank, following the army's example, and from 1939 also included piping that identified the branch of service. The collar tabs initially bore only the *sigrunen* for the *Leibstandarte* and an additional Latin number for the *Standarte* or the emblem of the special *Sturmbanne*, such as the pioneers or signals *Sturmbann*. In the *SS-Totenkopf-Verbände* the collar tab initially bore the Death's Head plus the number of the *Hundertschaft*. The *Totenkopf* collar tab underwent a number of changes over the course of time, which will be examined briefly in the subsequent text.

The constantly growing demand for insignia led to a broad production spectrum. The emblems for the organizations of the NSDAP (National Socialist German Workers Party), including those for the *Waffen-SS*, were made by many small and large firms to standards set by the *Reichszeugmeisterei* (RZM = Reich Quartermaster's Office). Initially the badges differed in embroidered and woven versions. According to rank, collar tabs or cuff titles, for example, were machine-embroidered or woven or embroidered by hand using stronger aluminum thread (referred to as flat wire in collector circles). With respect to cuff titles and sleeve shields, the Ewald Vorsteher Ribbon Factory (BeVo) in Wuppertal was particularly well known, as it generally wove its company name into the product. It was, however, far from the only company that wove badges with the approval of the RZM. In addition to embroidered and woven versions, from 1944 there was also a simple printed cloth version of the sleeve shield. Further time and cost savings were scarcely possible by then. As well, badges were also produced in the home countries of SS volunteers—for example in Belgium and the Baltic States—in some cases by the men themselves, according to RZM specifications. These often differed from badges produced in Germany, however.

The regulations for designing new badges became ever more detailed. Collar tabs were introduced which bore political symbols instead of *Sigrunen*, on the one hand to outwardly show that the decorated SS member was part of an elite, and on the other to respond to volunteers who were not sympathetic to the SS (*Note*: Until the special insignia were issued, the SS volunteers either wore the *Sigrunen* or no emblem at all on their right collar tab—as in the *Sicherheitsdienst der SS* (SS Security Service or SD). The sleeve shields also indicated the wearer's racial origins—usually by displaying national colors. In making up nation shields, the *Waffen-SS* came up with its own design, which differed from the very curved style used by the *Wehrmacht*. As more than a few foreign volunteers transferred to the *Waffen-SS*, retaining their former nation shields, there was a wide variety of styles to be seen.

There was similar diversity in the numerous cuff titles and in advance of this also in the designations of the SS divisions. It is impossible to say which criteria Himmler and the *SS-Hauptamt* used to decide which unit received which name and also which should receive a corresponding cuff title and which should not. The fundamental reason for awarding a name was to create an *esprit de corps*. Of the forty SS divisions, however, only twenty-eight were given a name, and furthermore, only nineteen received one or more cuff titles. As an example there was the *6. SS-Gebirgs-Division "Nord,"* which, though it bore the name "*Nord*," never received a cuff title with that name. Nevertheless many members of the division wore such a title, obtaining one from the *SS-Oberabschnitt "Nord"* of the *Allgemeine-SS*. The *13. Waffen-Gebirgs-Division der SS (kroatische Nr. 1)* was given the name "*Handschar*" but likewise received no cuff title. On the other hand, cuff titles were at least made for the *21. Waffen-Gebirgs-Division der SS "Skanderbeg" (albanische Nr. 1)*, which was formed a year later, but in the end were not issued. The *19. (lettische Nr. 2)* and *20. Waffen-Grenadier-Division der SS (estnische Nr. 1)*, which in contrast to the previously named Balkan divisions had a much greater fighting strength, were not given division names. But one can also not say that the new formations created from 1943—for the most part from ethnic Germans or foreigners—were given names, even though in some cases it was obvious from Himmler's speeches that he had doubts about their morale. In any case, units like the *14. Waffen-Grenadier-Division der SS (galizische Nr. 1)* or the *30. Waffen-Grenadier-Division der SS (russische Nr. 2)* were not given names but failed completely in the field. Perhaps Himmler assumed that the East-Europeans first had to earn a name through courageous action.

As one can see, the wearing of insignia was extremely varied. Furthermore, during the second half of the war it was only possible to achieve the uniform appearance of troops, even within the same unit, during the formation of new units. In this regard the recollections of a former member of the *SS-Totenkopf-Division*, who described the subject of insignia from his own viewpoint, will conclude the introduction:

> At the beginning of the war I still belonged to the *2. SS-Totenkopf-Standarte "Brandenburg"* and wore the *"Brandenburg"* cuff title plus the Totenkopf collar tab with our Hundertschaft number. When we moved to Dachau after the Polish Campaign, we had to remove our insignia

and were given a collar tab on which only the Death's Head was to be seen. Then, before the campaign in France, new collar tabs were issued which had Death's Heads on both sides. Then, prior to the Russian Campaign, new collar tabs were again issued, with the Death's Head on the right one and the rank on the left one as before. When division commander "Papa" Eicke was killed during a reconnaissance flight in a Fieseler Storch, the entire division volunteered to recover him. Our regiment then received his name "*Theodor Eicke*" and we a cuff title that we were supposed to sew onto our service coats. If one got along well with the company tailor, he did it. Just as in the replacing of collar tabs after promotions; one did not just receive new shoulder straps but a new left collar tab as well—at first one also got one for the greatcoat. Later they merely pressed braid or stars for the collar tabs into one's hand and one had to see to it himself that one was optically upgraded. Whereas in the beginning we all had the same cuff titles, increasingly this changed as a result of the arrival of replacements and transfers. Recruits came to us without cuff titles and our clothing NCO had none to give out. As far as men who were transferred to us from another unit, who already wore some sort of cuff title, they were supposed to remove them and apply the new ones. But the same question arose as before; where to get them? The officers had it easier. They could order their badges through the clothing stores. If we had the opportunity to go on leave, we could purchase what we needed in a uniform store. But first of all there was no more leave and second the thought never entered our heads. We preferred to spend the 1 mark 50 *pfennig* we got per day on other things. And so we went around in what we had, and until the end of the war that wasn't much.

CAP BADGES

Early eagle for the *SS-Schaftmütze* (service cap).

In addition to the *Waffen-SS* version of the eagle introduced in 1936, it was not unusual for officers to wear the army national emblem on their caps or sleeves (see pages 18 and 37).

The first version of the Death's Head cap emblem was identical to the one worn by the men of the Royal Prussian *1. Leibhusaren-Regiment Nr. 1 (Totenkopf-Reiter)* of Danzig on their service caps and visorless field caps. It was officially replaced by the second version (right) in 1936 but continued in use until 1941 (see photo of *SS-Unterscharführer* Rudi Kirchner at right).

Death's Head second version.

Cap eagle, embroidered.

Death's Head for garrison cap—woven version.

A trapezoidal badge for the standard garrison cap was introduced in 1943 and as with most badges there were embroidered and woven versions (the woven version for the black garrison cap of the *SS-Panzertruppen* is shown here).

SLEEVE EAGLES

Italy was only country that provided volunteers for the *Waffen-SS* that was given the right to add its national emblem—the fasces—to the uniform.

The first version of the SS sleeve eagle was introduced in 1935.

The second version—here for officers—followed in 1936 (hand-embroidered metal thread).

Initially the sleeve eagle emblem for the Italian SS Legion was embroidered or woven on a red field. The woven version is seen here.

Eagle for other ranks—embroidered rayon.

There were machine-woven eagles for other ranks in white and yellow rayon.

In the summer of 1944, the first SS formations began receiving an eagle on black cloth. Here is the hand-embroidered version for officers.

Yellow rayon was used for tropical clothing. There were embroidered and woven versions, but none for officers!

From 1944, eagle emblems for officers were machine-woven using thin metal thread.

Woven version of the eagle for other ranks of the *29. SS Waffen Grenadier Division der SS (italienische Nr. 1)*.

COLLAR TABS

Collar tab with embroidered runes for non-commissioned officers and enlisted men (rayon).

Woven runes (rayon) for non-commissioned officers and enlisted men.

In 1940–41, officers sometimes wore *sigrunen* on both collar tabs.

Woven collar tab with thin metal thread (flat wire).

Collar tab, hand-embroidered with metal thread, for officers to the rank of *SS-Standartenführer*.

SS-Schütze Hans Widmer.

Collar tabs for, from top to bottom:

SS-Schütze
SS-Sturmmann (*Gefreiter*)
SS-Rottenführer
(*Obergefreiter*)
SS-Unterscharführer
(*Unteroffizier*)

SS-Sturmmann Wilhelm Barenscheer.

Seen here as an *SS-Rottenführer*, Willi Rogmann was later awarded the Close Combat Bar in Gold.

SS-Unterscharführer Hans Erlewein.

While a member of the *SS-Panzergrenadier-Regiment "Westland," SS-Scharführer* Georg Duiker wore a metal "W" on his shoulder straps.

Collar tab for an *SS-Scharführer* (*Unterfeldwebel*).

SS-Hauptscharführer Fred Zura.

SS-Oberscharführer (*Feldwebel*).

SS-Sturmscharführer (*Stabsfeldwebel*).

SS-Hauptscharführer (*Oberfeldwebel*).

SS-Untersturmführer (*Leutnant*).

SS-Obersturmführer Erich Kühbandner, wearer of the Anti-Partisan War Badge in Gold.

SS-Untersturmführer Butte.

SS-Obersturmführer (*Oberleutnant*).

SS-Hauptsturmführer (*Hauptmann*).

SS-Hauptsturmführer Putmann-Cramer.

SS-Obersturmbannführer Stadler's decorations included the Close Combat Bar in Gold.

Collar tabs for an *SS-Sturmbannführer* (*Major*).

Hugo Kraas, last commander of the *12. SS-Panzer-Division "Hitlerjugend."*

Collar tabs for an *SS-Obersturmbannführer* (*Oberstleutnant*).

From the rank of *SS-Obersturmbannführer* (*Oberstleutnant*) rank badges were worn on both collar tabs.

In 1942, the collar tabs of the *Waffen-SS* from the rank of *SS-Oberführer* were modified. Not only were they changed visually by stitching the oak leaves in a straight instead of slightly curved form, but the number of stars on the collar tabs—from the rank of *SS-Brigadeführer*—was also changed to match those on the shoulder boards.

SS-Oberführer Wagner with the first version of the collar tab for *SS-Oberführer*.

SS-Oberführer Fegelein with the second version of the collar tab for *SS-Oberführer*.

Collar tabs for an *SS-Oberführer* as of 1942.

SS-Brigadeführer Georg Keppler wearing the first version of the collar tab for *SS-Brigadeführer*: two oak leaves and one star.

From left to right: *SS-Sturmbannführer* Temme, *SS-Brigadeführer* Fegelein and *SS-Standartenführer* Lombard. Note the different insignia in metal and fabric on their caps.

Collar tabs for an *SS-Brigadeführer* and *Generalmajor der Waffen-SS* in the style introduced in 1942.

SS-Gruppenführer and *Generalleutnant der Waffen-SS* Walter Krüger during the fighting at the Mius River, where he commanded the *2. SS-Panzer-Grenadier-Division "Das Reich."*

Collar tabs for an *SS-Gruppenführer* in the style introduced in 1942.

Here Theodor Eicke is wearing the early style collar tabs for *SS-Gruppenführer* with three oak leaves. Also note the Death's Head diamond.

Here Sepp Dietrich is still wearing the first version of the collar tab for an *SS-Obergruppenführer* with three oak leaves and one star.

SS-Obergruppenführer and *General der Waffen-SS und Polizei* von dem Bach, whose decorations included the Knight's Cross of the Iron Cross, the German Cross in Gold, and the Anti-Partisan War Badge, was appointed commander of anti-partisan units on June 21, 1943.

Collar tabs for an *SS-Obergruppenführer* and *General der Waffen-SS* in the style introduced in 1942.

Sepp Dietrich—promoted to *SS-Oberst-Gruppenführer* and *Panzer-Generaloberst der Waffen-SS* on August 1, 1944—was a wearer of the Knight's Cross of the Iron Cross with Oak Leaves, Swords and Diamonds.

The rank title was written in two parts to prevent confusion with the rank of *SS-Obergruppenführer*.

Collar tabs for an *SS-Oberst-Gruppenführer*.

Heinrich Himmler was *Reichsführer-SS* from January 6, 1929 until April 29, 1945. Even though this position did not represent any rank in the *Waffen-SS*, it is included because of his close association with the *Waffen-SS*.

Collar tabs for the *Reichsführer-SS*.

In 1940, *SS-Sturmmann* Willi Oswald (left)—note the *SS-Heimwehr Danzig* pin of honor on his breast pocket—wore the Death's Head on both collar tabs, in contrast to the members of *SS-Totenkopf-Standarte 10* (right), who in 1939 had the Death's Head on the right collar tab only.

Hand-embroidered metal thread.

Right: Woven version in the style introduced in April 1941.

Embroidered version in the style introduced in April 1941.

Helmut Upphoff

The *SS-Totenkopf-Standarten* initially wore the forwards-facing Death's Head—in some cases on both collar tabs, beginning in the spring of 1940. In 1941, the men of the *SS-Totenkopf-Division* received a new collar tab, on which the Death's Head was turned to the right.

SS-Standartenführer Goetze wearing the forwards-facing Death's Head on both collar tabs during the Western Campaign in 1940.

For a time, officers—here members of *SS-Infanterie-Regiment 10 (mot.)*—were permitted to wear the collar tab with the Death's Head looking right, which was introduced in April 1941, on both collar tabs.

From the time of its formation until it was absorbed by the *Waffen-SS* in February 1942, members of the *SS-Polizei-Division* (SS Police Division) wore the SS eagle on the sleeve along with the *Schutzpolizei* collar tab. All effects of the *Waffen-SS* were subsequently introduced, as well as the cuff title of the *SS-Polizei-Division* (see photo below right).

Collar tab for non-commissioned officers and enlisted men.

Collar tab for officers of the *SS-Polizei-Division* until February 1942. Note the runes beneath the left breast pockets in the photo on the left, which identify the men as members of the SS.

Approximately 200,000 ethnic Germans—primarily from Rumania, Hungary, Croatia, Serbia, Poland and Slovakia—served in existing *Waffen-SS* divisions or formed their own units. As only a part of these men met the criteria set by the SS, they did not wear SS runes, instead wearing special collar tabs.

The Odal Rune of the *7. SS-Freiwilligen-Gebirgs-Division "Prinz Eugen."*

From left to right: *SS-Obersturmbannführer* Petersen, wearing the Odal Rune on both collar tabs, *SS-Obergruppenführer* Phleps, *SS-Sturmbannführer* Dietsche and *SS-Standartenführer* Kumm.

The collar tab of the *24. Waffen-Gebirgs [Karstjäger]-Division der SS* features a karst thistle. The division, formed from residents of the Adriatic coastal region, never had more than 2,000 men.

A Norwegian *SS-Rottenführer* of the *11. SS-Freiwilligen-Panzergrenadier-Division "Nordland"* with the sun wheel on his collar tab and the national shield on his upper left arm.

While the *Freikorps "Danmark"* generally wore the *sigrunen*, in Denmark itself the replacement company wore a special collar tab with the Danish flag (*Danebrog*). A closed sun wheel was envisaged for the *SS-Panzergrenadier-Regiment 24 "Danmark"* but was never introduced.

In order to counter the growing partisan threat in the Balkans, the Germans began recruiting Muslim Croats for the *13. Waffen-Gebirgs-Division der SS "Handschar" (kroat Nr. 1)* and the *23. Waffen-Gebirgs-Division der SS "Kama" (kroat Nr. 2)*. Like the *21. Waffen-Gebirgs-Division der SS "Skanderbeg"* formed in Albania, they proved of little use to Germany.

The "*Handschar*" (curved sword) of the *13. Waffen-Gebirgs-Division der SS "Handschar" (kroatische Nr. 1)*.

The helmet of the Albanian national hero Skanderbeg on the collar tab of the *21. Waffen-Gebirgs-Division der SS "Skanderbeg"(albanische Nr. 1)*.

Together with a shield, the kindshal—the traditional Caucasian weapon—formed the symbol of the Caucasian *Waffen-Verband* of the SS.

The collar tab with the wolf's head—the symbol of the Gök-Turks, ancestors of the men who served in the East-Turkish *Waffen-Verband* of the SS.

The lion, the Galician heraldic animal, on the collar tab of the *14. Waffen-Grenadier-Division der SS (ukrainische Nr. 1)*.

The collar tab for the *20. Waffen-Grenadier-Division der SS "RONA" (russische Nr. 1)* with the Cross of St. George.

The White-Ruthenian double cross on the collar tab of the *30. Waffen-Grenadier-Division der SS (weißruthenische Nr. 1)*.

Approximately 20,000 West Ukrainians from Galicia served in the *14. Waffen-Grenadier-Division der SS (ukrainische Nr. 1)* during the two years of its existence. As well, approximately 15,000 Russians served in the *29.* and *30. Waffen-Grenadier-Division der SS (russische Nr. 1* and *2)*, at least briefly. The combat value of these units was minimal.

After the contracts of many Baltic volunteers serving in the *Wehrmacht* and police expired in 1942, the *Waffen-SS* began recruiting them for service in its ranks. The units reached division strength in 1943 and often fought energetically against the Red Army. Approximately 40,000 Latvians and 20,000 Estonians served in the *Waffen-SS* by the end of the war.

Collar tab of the *15. Waffen-Grenadier-Division der SS (lett. Nr. 1)* with the symbolized rising sun and three stars for the Latvian lands: Courland, Livonia and Latgale.

The Latvian "*Ugunskrusts*" (Fire Cross) on the collar tab of the *19. Waffen-Grenadier-Division der SS (lettische Nr. 2)*.

Two versions of collar tab were used by the *20. Waffen-Grenadier-Division der SS (estnische Nr. 1)*. On one (see pay book photo) a knight's hand holds the sword next to the "E" for Estonia, while on the other the sword is alone next to the "E" (see collar tab right).

The SA rune of the *18. Freiwilligen-Panzergrenadier-Division "Horst Wessel"* was seldom worn. The unit's personnel did not come from the SA, as planned, but were ethnic Germans from Hungary.

The *22. SS-Freiwilligen-Kavallerie-Division*, which was also composed largely of ethnic Germans from Hungary, was given a collar tab with a cornflower, a symbol of the Danube Swabians.

In 1940, the *Waffen-SS* formed a special unit made up of convicted poachers, which was to become known as *SS-Sonderkommando "Dirlewanger."* The unit received a special collar tab at the beginning of 1943: two crossed rifles over a stick hand grenade. In 1945, the former *SS-Sonderkommando* formed the foundation of the *36. Waffen-Grenadier-Division der SS*.

Approximately 14,000 Dutchmen served in the *Waffen-SS*: about 2,000 were attached to the *SS-Division "Wiking"* and 6,000 each served in the *SS-Freiwilligen-Panzergrenadier-Brigade "Nederland"* (later *23. SS-Freiwilligen-Panzergrenadier-Division "Nederland"*) and the *34. SS-Freiwilligen-Grenadier-Division "Landstorm Nederland."*

The *Wolfsangel* (Wolf's Hook) was used by the *Freiwilligen-Legion "Niederlande"*—albeit horizontally—and later—vertically—by the *23. SS-Freiwilligen-Panzergrenadier-Division "Nederland" (niederl. Nr. 1)*.

A collar tab with an exploding shell was supposed to be introduced for use by the *34. SS-Freiwilligen-Grenadier-Division "Landstorm Nederland."* In fact, however, the volunteers wore either the *Wolfsangel* or normal *Sigrunen*.

The *Freiwilligen-Legion "Norwegen"* was originally supposed to wear a Viking ship on its collar tabs (illustration right). The Norwegians rejected this, however, and so soon afterwards a collar tab with the lion from the Norwegian coat of arms (illustration below) was introduced.

"Fight for Norway"

Members of the *Freiwilligen-Legion "Norwegen"* parade through Oslo—without weapons.

In contrast to other formations, for propaganda reasons the handful of members of the British Free Corps briefly wore collar tabs with the three lions of the English coat of arms.

Collar tabs with the letter "H" for Hungary of the *25.* and *26. Waffen-Grenadier-Division der SS "Hunyadi"* and *"Hungaria"* were—like their equipment and arms—only issued in small quantities.

The three-shanked sun wheel was initially worn by the *Freiwilligen-Legion "Flandern,"* then by the *SS-Sturmbrigade "Langemarck"* and finally by the *27. SS-Freiwilligen-Grenadier-Division "Langemarck" (flämische Nr. 1)*. In contrast to most other divisions formed in 1944, this collar tab was worn almost exclusively.

Collar tabs with crossed Burgundian knives were supposed to be introduced for the *28. SS-Freiwilligen-Grenadier-Division "Wallonien."* In the end, they were as rare as those of the *33. Waffen-Grenadier-Division der SS "Charlemagne"* with the sword of the "Maid of Orleans" (Joan of Arc) surrounded by two laurel leaves.

Flemish Knight's Cross holder Remy Schrijnen.

Among the nations that provided volunteers for the *Waffen-SS*, a special place was reserved for Italy. Hitler and Himmler obviously wanted to assure the Italian Socialist Republic (RSI) founded by Mussolini a visible "sovereignty" and so the approximately 6,000 Italians who ultimately served in the *Waffen-SS* were initially given the right to use red cloth for their badges. In the summer of 1944, standard collar tabs on black cloth were also issued, and at the end of the year the Italians received their own collar tabs, which like all *Waffen-SS* badges for foreign volunteers had no Sig-Runen but instead a symbol of their own, in this case the fasces. It is interesting that, in contrast to most other collar tabs, a second color—red, the color of martyrs—was embroidered in.

In the summer of 1944, approximately 20,000 members of the *Wehrmacht* were transferred to the concentration camps' *SS-Wachsturmbanne* to guard the approximately 100,000 to 200,000 Hungarian Jews expected to arrive for work in the armaments industry. To differentiate these new guard personnel from members of the *SS-Totenkopf* units, they were given their own collar tab with a double-armed swastika (below).

A collar tab for the planned *Waffen-Grenadier-Division der SS (rumänische)* with the emblem of the Rumanian Iron Guard was manufactured but not issued. As a rule, the approximately 3,000 Rumanian SS volunteers wore a plan black collar tab with no insignia.

SHOULDER STRAPS & SHOULDER BOARDS

Erich Rommel is promoted to *SS-Unterscharführer* on April 20, 1944.

SS-Kanonier to *SS-Rottenführer* of the *Nebelwerfer* (rocket launcher) troops.

SS-Unterscharführer of the artillery.

SS-Scharführer of the LAH (peacetime version).

A member of the German core personnel attached to the *13. Waffen-Gebirgs-Division der SS "Handschar" (kroatische Nr. 1)* with the rank of *SS-Sturmscharführer*. The *edelweiss* emblem on the right sleeve and the national shield on the left upper arm are clearly visible.

SS-Oberscharführer of the cavalry.

SS-Hauptscharführer of the reconnaissance troops.

SS-Sturmscharführer of the mountain infantry.

Cloth patches with the first letters or numbers of units were worn until about 1942. Officers and non-commissioned officers attached metal versions to their shoulder boards. Illustrated here are "G" for *Germania* and "W" for *Westland*.

An interesting photo of members of the *2. SS-Panzer-Division "Das Reich."* The *SS-Untersturmführer* is wearing the army eagle on his arm, while the *SS-Hauptscharführer* (Fred Zura) with the dog has the "piston rings," which identify him as a *Stabsscharführer* (senior NCO).

SS-Untersturmführer of the signals troops.

SS-Obersturmführer of the cavalry.

SS-Hauptsturmführer of the mountain troops.

SS-Oberführer Dr. Oskar Dirlewanger (note the first version of the collar tab for *SS-Oberführer*), commander of the notorious *SS-Sonderkommando "Dirlewanger."*

Shoulder board for *SS-Standartenführer* and *SS-Oberführer* of the pioneers.

Shoulder board for *SS-Obersturmbannführer* of the cavalry.

Shoulder board for *SS-Sturmbannführer* of the reconnaissance units.

Sepp Dietrich, seen here as an *SS-Obergruppenführer* and *General der Waffen-SS*.

Shoulder board for an *SS-Oberst-Gruppenführer* and *Generaloberst der Waffen-SS*.

Shoulder board for an *SS-Brigadeführer* and *Generalmajor der Waffen-SS*.

Shoulder board for an *SS-Obergruppenführer* and *General der Waffen-SS*.

UPPER ARM RANK BADGES

Star for *SS-Oberschützen*.

SS-Oberschütze Wendel, who, as one of the first members of "*Prinz Eugen,*" initially wore no *sigrunen* collar tab.

Chevrons for *SS-Sturmmänner* (above left) and *SS-Rottenführer* (above right)—there was no *Waffen-SS* badge patterned after that of the army's *Stabsgefreiten* (two chevrons and one star): after at least six years of service, however, *SS-Rottenführer* were eligible for a higher pay grade.

SS-Unterscharführer

SS-Scharführer

The so-called rank badges for officers and non-commissioned officers of the *Waffen-SS* on articles of clothing without shoulder boards or shoulder straps were similar to those used by the army and were usually manufactured using the textile printing method, although some were made by sewing of braid in combination with embroidery.

SS-Oberscharführer

SS-Hauptscharführer

SS-Sturmscharführer

SS-Untersturmführer

SS-Obersturmführer

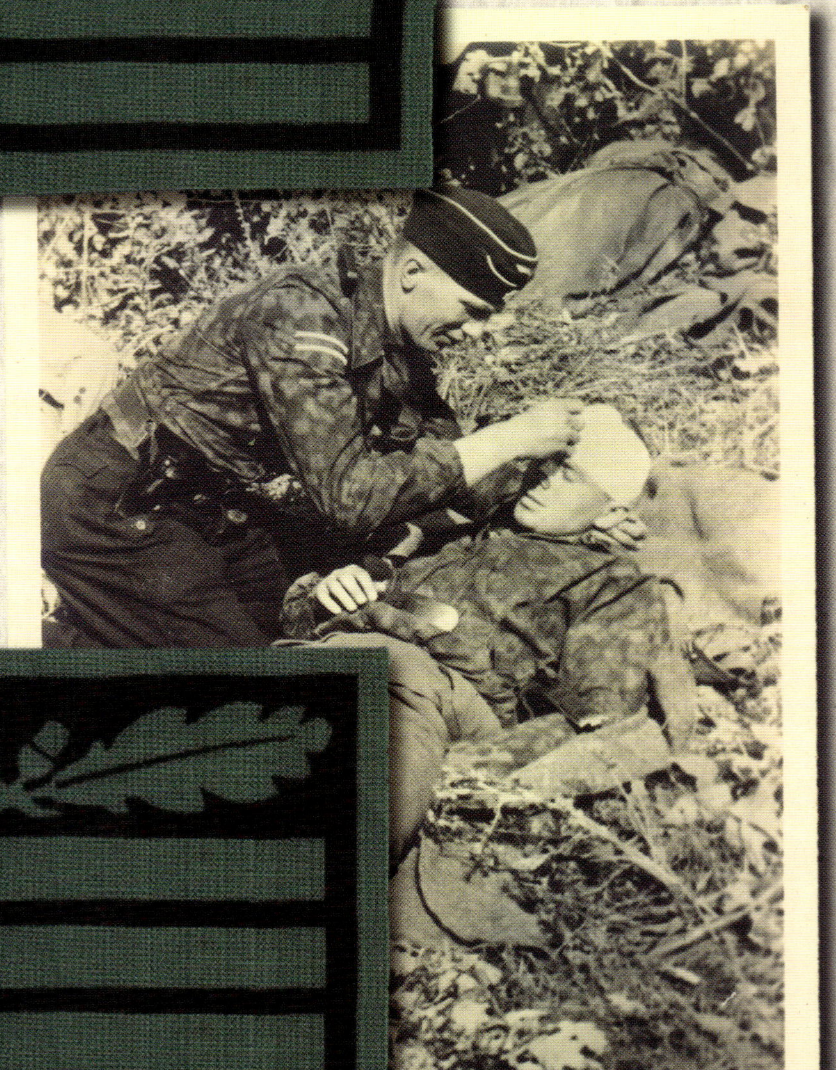

In February 1943, the *Waffen-SS* adopted the upper arm rank badges introduced by the *Wehrmacht* in autumn 1942. Previously it had used strips of braid approximately ten centimeters long: one braid for non-commissioned officers and two for officers.

SS-Hauptsturmführer

SS-Sturmbannführer

SS-Obersturmbannführer

SS-Standartenführer

SS-Oberführer, a rank that had no equivalent in the *Wehrmacht*.

SS-Brigadeführer

SS-Gruppenführer

SS-Obergruppenführer

SS-Oberst-Gruppenführer

ARM SHIELDS

Approximately 1,500 Finns served in the *Waffen-SS* until July 1943. The men of the so-called Finnish Battalion (*III./ SS-Panzergrenadier-Regiment "Nordland"*) wore the Finnish Lion on the left forearm.

A rectangular national shield was initially worn in the *Freiwilligen-Legion "Norwegen."*

Approximately 3,000 Danes joined the *Waffen-SS*: of these about half were from the German ethnic group in Northern Schleswig.

Approximately 3,500 Norwegians served in the *Waffen-SS* and wore a national shield in Norway's national colors.

The Dutch national shield was worn first by the *Freiwilligen-Legion "Niederlande,"* then from 1943 by the *SS-Freiwilligen-Panzergrenadier-Brigade "Nederland"* and finally from 1945 in the *23. SS-Freiwilligen-Panzergrenadier-Division "Nederland" (niederl. Nr.* 1). The *34. SS-Freiwilligen-Grenadier-Division "Landstorm Nederland" (niederl. Nr. 2)* wore no national shield, probably because the unit was only deployed in its Dutch homeland.

Himmler had an interest in taking the Flemings into the SS early on. In addition to the Flemings in the *SS-Division "Wiking,"* the *Freiwilligen-Legion "Flandern"* was formed in 1941. In 1943, bolstered by Flemish armaments workers, it formed the *SS-Freiwilligen-Sturmbrigade "Langemarck."* In 1944, this was expanded to form the *27. SS-Freiwilligen-Grenadier-Division "Langemarck" (flämische Nr. 1).*

In May 1943, the *Waffen-SS* took over the Walloons serving in the army and formed the *SS-Freiwilligen-Sturmbrigade "Wallonien,"* which was later expanded into the *28. SS-Freiwilligen-Grenadier-Division "Wallonien."* Interestingly, its roughly 4,500 men retained the *Wehrmacht* national shield.

The *Waffen-SS* began forming a French SS-Regiment in the summer of 1943, which bit by bit was expanded into the *33. Waffen-Grenadier-Division der SS "Charlemagne" (französische Nr. 1)* by taking in French volunteers in the *Wehrmacht*. The total of just under 10,000 members were supposed to wear the *tricolore* on the lower right sleeve.

National shield for members of the *13. Waffen-Gebirgs-Division der SS "Handschar" (kroat Nr. 1)* and the short-lived *23. Waffen-Grenadier-Division der SS "Kama" (kroatische Nr. 2)*.

National shield with the Albanian two-headed eagle of the *21. Waffen-Gebirgs-Division der SS "Skanderbeg" (albanische Nr. 1)*.

About 400 Spaniards—most members of the disbanded *250. Infanterie-Division*—did not follow Franco's order to return to Spain, instead voluntarily continuing to serve on the German side from the spring of 1944. About half formed a company that was attached to the *5. SS-Freiwilligen-Sturmbrigade "Wallonien."*

About 124,000 Latvians served in German units from 1941, approximately 40,000 of them in two divisions of the *Waffen-SS*. Like all foreign formations, there were many variations in uniforms and badges, as the photo of two Latvian SS volunteers taken in 1943 shows. On the right the national shield introduced for the *Waffen-SS* in 1944.

Harald Nugiseks was awarded the Knight's Cross on April 9, 1944 while serving with the *20. Waffen-Grenadier-Division der SS (estnische Nr. 1)*. The colorized photo illustrates well how the national shield was worn and the special collar tab.

National shield for the approximately fifty members of the British Free Corps, the so-called "Union Jack."

The arm shield worn by the Italian volunteers of the *29. Waffen-Grenadier-Division der SS (ital. Nr. 1)* bore the fasces (fascist symbol) instead of the national colors.

In the summer of 1944, the *Waffen-SS* took over the approximately 3,000 Indians serving in the army's *Infanterie-Regiment 950* and formed the *Indische Legion der Waffen-SS*. While a new collar tab with an embroidered tiger and SS belt buckles and arm eagles were introduced, the army national shield remained unchanged.

The Kaminski Brigade was formed within the *2. Panzer-Armee* in 1941, and in 1944 the Senior SS and Police Commander "Russia-Center and White Ruthenia" took over the brigade, which called itself the Russian People's Liberation Army (RONA). The brigade was taken into the *Waffen-SS* on July 31, 1944 and was supposed to form the basis of the *29. Waffen-Grenadier-Division der SS "RONA" (russische Nr. 1)*.

An extensive recruiting campaign was begun in Galicia in 1943, as a result of which approximately 20,000 volunteers were recruited for the formation of the *Galizischen SS-Freiwilligen-Division* (Galician SS Volunteer Division) and SS police regiments. Little by little these were also taken into the later *14. Waffen-Grenadier-Division der SS (ukrainische Nr. 1)*. All wore the coat of arms of Galicia.

Plans to form a *Waffen-Grenadier-Division der SS (bulgariche)* in November 1944 failed. Only about 1,000 Bulgarians tuned up at the Döllersheim troop training grounds in Lower Austria for formation of the *Waffen-Grenadier-Regiment der SS (bulgarisches)*. It saw no action and surrendered to the western Allies.

Formation of the *25. Waffen-Grenadier-Division der SS "Hunyadi" (ungar. Nr. 1)* began in November 1944 and the *26. Waffen-Grenadier-Division der SS "Hungaria" (ungar. Nr. 2)* followed in December. Altogether, more than 40,000 Hungarians served in the *Waffen-SS*. There were serious problems in equipping the units and this included badges: the illustration shows the planned arm shield, which was never introduced.

At the end of 1944, the *1.* and *2. SS-Kosaken-Kavallerie-Division* were formed using about 25,000 Cossacks, most taken from the *Wehrmacht*. The regiments wore the arm shields they had used in the *Wehrmacht* with Cyrillic letters:

TB (Latin TW = *Terekskoye Voysko* = Terek Regiment) with black-blue shield
KB (Latin KW = *Kubanskoye Voysko* = Kuban Regiment) with black-red shield
ВД (Latin WD = *Voysko Donskoye* = Don Regiment) with blue-red shield
ПСВ (Latin PSW = *Polk Sibirskoye Voysko* = Siberian Regiment) with blue-yellow shield

In January 1944, the SS-FHA had plans to form an East-Muslim SS division in the Generalgouvernement (Poland). Its core was to be formed by the Turkestani *Infanterie-Bataillon 450*, which was taken over from the army. As the *Wehrmacht* rejected more extensive transfers of personnel and was itself never able to establish even a brigade, in June 1944 an *Ostmuselmanischen SS-Regiment 1* (East-Muslim SS Regiment 1) was formed, from which the East-Turkish *Waffen-Verband* of the SS was created in October 1944. This was organized into three *Waffen-Gruppen*: "*Idel-Ural*," "*Turkistan*" and "*Krim*," with a combined total of about 5,000 men.

The pay book of Turkestani *SS-Mann* Chalinmow in *Ostmuselmanische SS-Regiment 1*.

On December 30, 1944, the SS-FHA ordered the formation of the Caucasian *Waffen-Verband der SS*. Approximately 5,000 men, mostly former members of the Red Army from the Caucasus who had been captured and were now serving in the army or police, were taken into the *Waffen-SS*. The unit was organized into four battalion-size *Waffen-Gruppen*: "*Georgien*," "*Aserbaidschan*," "*Armenien*" and "*Nordkaukasien*" and were attached to the Supreme SS and Police Commander Italy for anti-partisan operations. The badges were woven or, more commonly, simply printed.

CUFF TITLES

Probably the best-known *Waffen-SS* cuff titles were those bearing the name "*Adolf Hitler*" and worn first by the *Leibstandarte* and later the *1. SS-Panzer-Division "LAH."* While other divisions also had cuff titles with the names of their regiments, the *Leibstandarte* kept just the one.

In addition to cuff titles bearing the division name (embroidered version for other ranks shown), within the *2. SS-Panzer-Division "Das Reich"* cuff titles were also worn with the name "*Deutschland*" in *SS-Panzergrenadier-Regiment 3* (embroidered version for other ranks shown) and *"Der Führer"* in *SS-Panzergrenadier-Regiment 4* (hand-embroidered version for officers shown).

The *3. SS-Panzer-Division "Totenkopf"* was originally formed mainly from members of the *SS-Totenkopf* units. In addition to the "*Totenkopf*" cuff title bearing the title or Death's Head emblem, members of *SS-Panzergrenadier-Regiment 6* wore the name of fallen (February 26, 1943) division commander Theodor Eicke (see below).

Woven "*Totenkopf*" cuff title.

Former members of the *1. SS-Totenkopf-Standarte "Oberbayern"* were permitted to wear a cuff title with Death's Head emblem (hand-embroidered version for officers shown).

The *SS-Heimwehr Danzig* was formed in the summer of 1939 and in autumn 1939 it was taken into *SS-Totenkopf-Infanterie-Regiment 3* of the *SS-Totenkopf-Division* as a complete battalion. Its members were permitted to wear the *SS-Heimwehr Danzig* cuff title as a commemorative badge.

Although it was initially formed as a police division within the army, in the summer of 1940 the unit was given the prefix "SS-." Then on February 10, 1942 it was officially incorporated into the *Waffen-SS*. Designated *SS-Polizei-Panzergrenadier-Division* from April 1943, in October 1943 it became the 4th SS Division of the *Waffen-SS* during the renumbering of its units. The *SS-Polizei-Division* cuff title introduced in April 1942 was worn until the end of the war. The woven version is shown here.

SS-Gruppenführer Gille, commanding officer of the *5. SS-Panzer-Division "Wiking"* (left), with the hand-embroidered version of the cuff title.

Three cuff titles were worn within the *5. SS-Panzer-Division "Wiking"*: in addition to the obligatory "*Wiking*" (embroidered version for other ranks shown), *SS-Panzergrenadier-Regiment 9* wore the title "*Germania*" (hand-embroidered version for officers shown) and *SS-Panzergrenadier-Regiment 10* the title "*Westland*" (embroidered version for other ranks shown).

Reinhard Heydrich

Michael Gaißmair

SS-Sturmmann Willi Wind

Interestingly, the *6. SS-Gebirgs-Division "Nord,"* which had its origins in *SS-Kampfgruppe "Nord,"* had no cuff title with the division name, in order to avoid confusion with *SS-Oberabschnitt "Nord"* of the *Allgemeine-SS*. In 1942, however, Hitler awarded the name of *SS-Obergruppenführer* Reinhard Heydrich, who died on May 28, 1942 after an assassination attempt, to *SS-Gebirgsjäger-Regiment 6*. On June 20, 1944, *SS-Gebirgsjäger-Regiment 12* was given the name of peasant leader "*Michael Gaißmair*."

Together with the earlier *SS-Totenkopf-Infanterie-Regimenter 6* and *7*, *SS-Totenkopf-Infanterie-Regiment 9* was deployed on the northern front. In December 1941, it was transferred to the Volkhov sector and simultaneously awarded the name "*Thule*." In August 1942, it was attached to the *SS-Totenkopf-Division* as the *Schnelles SS-Schützen-Regiment "Thule"* (Fast SS Rifle Regiment "Thule"). Despite frequent claims to the contrary, the name "Thule" was never awarded to *SS-Panzergrenadier-Regiment 5*.

Thule

Members of the *7. SS-Freiwilligen-Gebirgs-Division* only wore the "*Prinz Eugen*" cuff title. When the division commander was killed in September 1944, *SS-Freiwilligen-Gebirgsjäger-Regiment 13* was awarded the name "*Artur Phleps*," however no further cuff titles were produced. In the literature it is claimed now and then that *SS-Freiwilligen-Gebirgsjäger-Regiment 14* was awarded the name "*Skanderbeg*" after absorbing the remnants of the *21. Waffen-Gebirgs-Division der SS (albanische Nr. 1)*. This does not, however, correspond to facts and is pure conjecture.

Prinz Eugen

After Hitler awarded the *8. SS-Kavallerie-Division* the name "*Florian Geyer*" on March 12, 1944, corresponding cuff titles were issued, replacing the seldom-worn bands bearing the title "*SS-Kavallerie-Division.*"

Florian Geyer

The later *9. SS-Panzer-Division "Hohenstaufen"* was formed in early 1943 as a panzergrenadier division. Not all of its members had joined the *Waffen-SS* voluntarily. All of the division's units wore the "*Hohenstaufen*" cuff title. Here is the well-known version made by BeVo of Wuppertal for non-commissioned officers and enlisted men (other ranks).

Hohenstaufen

On December 19, 1942, Hitler ordered the formation of an *SS Panzergrenadier-Division*, which was initially called "*Karl der Große*." On October 26, 1943, it was renamed *10. SS-Panzer-Division "Frundsberg."*

Frundsberg

Two members of the *10. SS-Panzer-Division "Frundsberg."* Note that they are not wearing the triangle for SS signals personnel but instead the army-style badge on an oval base.

The majority of the *11. SS-Freiwilligen-Panzergrenadier-Division*'s personnel were ethnic Germans from Rumania—only about 10% were volunteers from Denmark and Norway. In addition to the "*Nordland*" cuff title, the names "*Norge*" and "*Danmark*" were worn in *SS-Freiwilligen-Panzergrenadier-Regiment 23* and *24* respectively. Members of *SS-Panzer-Abteilung 11* were issued cuff titles with the name "*Hermann von Salza*."

Nordland

Norge

Danmark

Hermann von Salza

Originally conceived for volunteers from the SA, ethnic Germans from Hungary made up the bulk of the *18. SS-Freiwilligen-Panzergrenadier-Division*, which on January 30, 1944, received the name "*Horst Wessel.*" The unit never reached its full combat strength before the end of the war.

In 1944, the *21. Waffen-Gebirgs-Division der SS "Skanderberg" (albanische Nr. 1)* was formed with the cooperation of the Albanian government and it briefly fought unsuccessfully against the partisans. This cuff title is woven with a thin metal thread (so-called flat wire).

The *5. SS-Freiwilligen-Panzergrenadier-Brigade "Nederland"* was created from the *Freiwilligen-Legion "Niederlande,"* which wore a cuff title with the same name, in the summer of 1943. In February 1945, it was supposed to have been expanded into the nominal *23. SS-Freiwilligen-Panzergrenadier-Division "Nederland" (niederländische Nr. 1)*. *SS-Freiwilligen-Panzergrenadier-Regiment 48* had previously received the name "*General Seyffardt*" on November 30, 1943 and *SS-Freiwilligen-Panzergrenadier-Regiment 49* the name "*de Ruiter*."

In the summer of 1943, formation began of an *SS-Panzergrenadier-Division* made up mainly of seventeen-year-old members of the Hitler Youth who had not yet begun their compulsory military service. In the autumn of that year the unit was renamed *12. SS-Panzer-Division "Hitlerjugend."*

Hitlerjugend

The *SS-Sturmbrigade "Reichsführer-SS"* was initially formed from the earlier *Begleit-Bataillon "Reichsführer-SS"* and finally, in autumn 1943, it became the *16. Panzergrenadier-Division* with the same name. Interestingly, the cuff title was not introduced into the division until relatively late.

Reichsführer-SS

Formation of the *17. SS-Panzergrenadier-Division* began in autumn 1943, and in April 1944, Hitler gave it the name "*Götz von Berlichingen*." The unit was used to defend against the invasion and was so badly mauled that it never regained full operational capability before the end of the war. The unit was made up of Reich and ethnic Germans.

Götz von Berlichingen

The "*Langemarck*" cuff title in the version woven from thin metal thread.

Langemarck

About 12,000 Belgians—divided between the two nationalities (Dutch-speaking Flemings and French-speaking Walloons) served in the *Waffen-SS*. The *Freiwilligen-Legion "Flandern"* ultimately became the *27. SS-Freiwilligen-Division "Langemarck" (flämische Nr. 1)* under the command of Konrad Schellong (left). Deployed separately, not until April 1945 were all the Belgians briefly combined into a battle group on the Oder Front.

Not until summer 1943 did Himmler allow Wallonian volunteers into the *Waffen-SS*. In February 1945, the *5. SS-Freiwilligen-Sturmbrigade "Wallonien"* became the *28. SS-Freiwilligen-Grenadier-Division "Wallonien" (wallonische Nr. 1)*. Only a few of its members wore cuff titles, however.

Wallonien

Charlemagne

The *Waffen-Grenadier-Brigade der SS "Charlemagne" (französische Nr. 1)* was formed in late summer 1944, and in February 1945 it was expanded into the 33. *Waffen-Grenadier-Division der SS "Charlemagne" (französische Nr. 1)*. Woven cuff titles were made but were not issued.

Landstorm Nederland

SS-Grenadier-Regiment 1 "Landstorm Nederland" was formed in autumn 1943 by taking in Dutch members of the *Ordnungspolizei*. It was subsequently expanded into a brigade, and in February 1945, the *34. Freiwilligen-Grenadier-Division "Landstorm Nederland" (niederl. Nr. 2)* was formed. Corresponding cuff titles were worn, at least in part

The cuff title "*SS-Feldgendarmerie*" was introduced in the summer of 1942 for the approximately 4,000 members of the *Waffen-SS* military police. Each major unit had from a squad to a company of military police. Here is a late version with woven metal thread. The *Kettenschild* or gorget (the military police were "*Kettenhunde*," or watchdogs, in soldier's parlance) and police national emblem were also worn.

Beginning in 1942, about 3,000 women between the ages of seventeen and thirty were trained as *SS-Nachrichtenmaiden* (female signals personnel) at the *Reichsschule-SS Oberrehnheim* and while there wore the cuff title "*Reichsschule-SS*."

Formation of the *Freiwilligen-Legionen* (Volunteer Legions) *"Flandern," "Niederlande"* and *"Norwegen"* and the *Freikorps "Danmark"* for the "struggle against bolshevism" began on November 6, 1941. Purely for propaganda reasons an attempt was made to make extensive use of cuff titles. The behavior of German core personnel, however, was often anything but a recruiting tool for service on the German side. Very few volunteers extended their commitment after their initial contracts expired.

From top to bottom, slightly reduced in size, are:

Embroidered cuff title of the *Freiwilligen-Legion "Niederlande"*

Embroidered cuff title of the *Freiwilligen-Legion "Norwegen"*

Woven cuff title (BeVo) of the *Freiwilligen-Legion "Flandern"*

Woven cuff title of the *Freikorps "Danmark"* (the term *Freikorps* was used because Denmark, unlike the other countries, was technically neutral).

Heinz Twesmann as a member of the *Freiwilligen-Legion "Norwegen."*

Frw. Legion Norwegen

Freiw. Legion Flandern

Freikorps Danmark

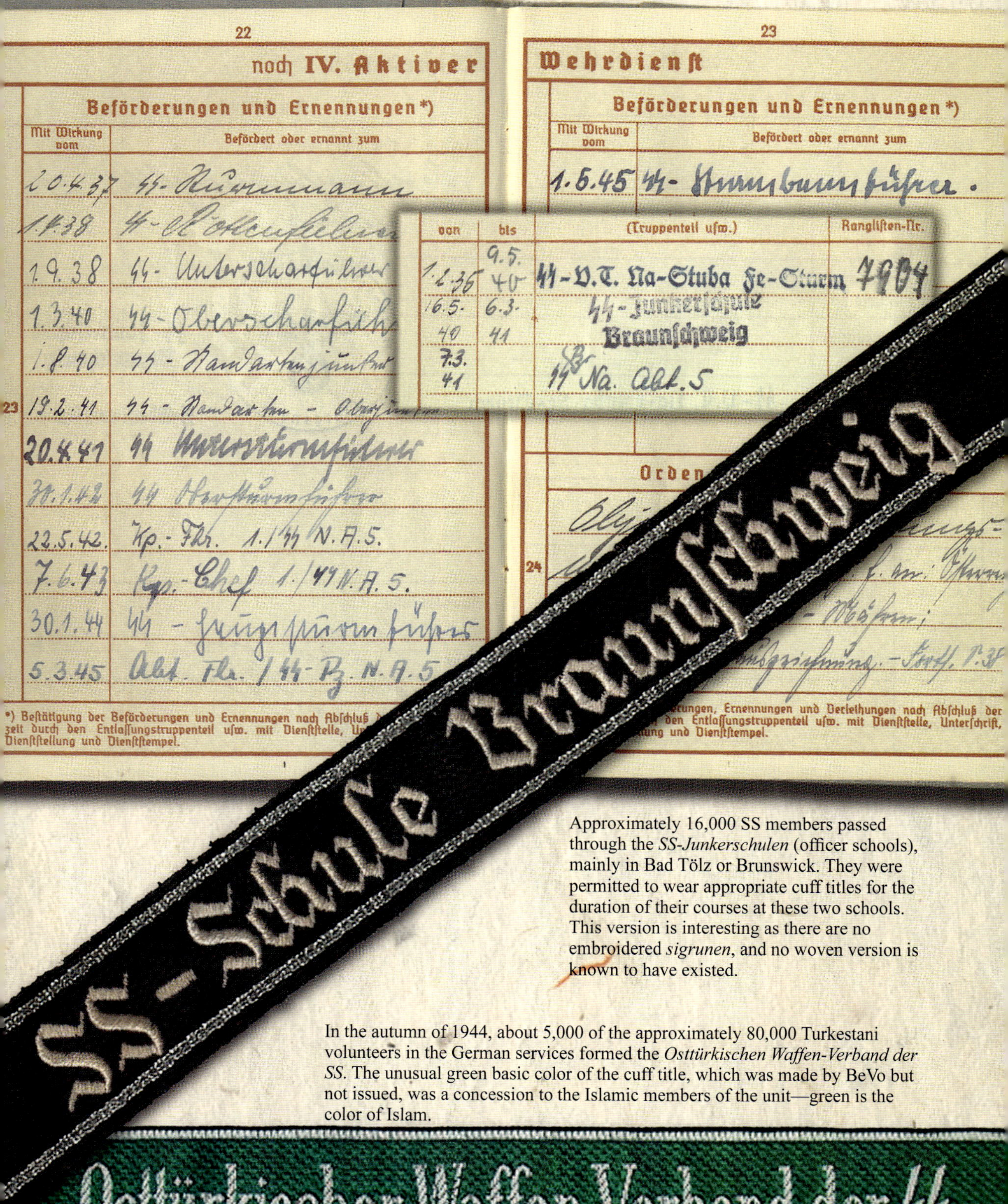

Approximately 16,000 SS members passed through the *SS-Junkerschulen* (officer schools), mainly in Bad Tölz or Brunswick. They were permitted to wear appropriate cuff titles for the duration of their courses at these two schools. This version is interesting as there are no embroidered *sigrunen*, and no woven version is known to have existed.

In the autumn of 1944, about 5,000 of the approximately 80,000 Turkestani volunteers in the German services formed the *Osttürkischen Waffen-Verband der SS.* The unusual green basic color of the cuff title, which was made by BeVo but not issued, was a concession to the Islamic members of the unit—green is the color of Islam.

SLEEVE DIAMONDS

As in the army, SS members of the special services were identified by special badges. Basically, in contrast to the army, these were to be in the form of black diamonds worn on the arm. There were badges for officer specialists detached from SS central offices to the *Waffen-SS*, which had no direct military reference. Finally, diamonds were also introduced to show that the man had previously been, for example, an NCO in the *Ordnungspolizei* or a leader in the Hitler Youth. These badges were little used, however.

An *SS-Unterscharführer* with the diamond for signals personnel (lightning bolt). Note the "*Nord*" cuff title, which was not officially introduced for the *6. SS-Gebirgs-Division*!

Diamond for medical personnel attached to first-aid units.

Pharmacist

General medical personnel

Veterinarian

Members of the workshop company of *SS-Panzer-Regiment 9 "Hohenstaufen."*

Schirrmeister (maintenance technical sergeant)

Sleeve diamond for weapons and equipment non-commissioned officers.

Shoeing personnel.

Beginning in the spring of 1942, the *Waffen-SS* introduced special diamond badges for officer and non-commissioned officer specialists.

In the *SS-Hauptamt*: recruiting and training, the "T" rune.

In the *Reichssicherheitshauptamt*: Race and Resettlement, the Odal rune and in SS and Police the *sigrunen* with police national emblem.

In the SS Economic and Administrative Central Office: Construction group the circle with star; and in the Enterprises Group the letter "W" with star (below); and officers in the administration just a star (bottom).

In the Reich Office for the Consolidation of German Nationhood: Settlement Group the eagle with plow and in the German Racial Assistance Office the cornflower.

From May 1943, non-commissioned officers of the *Ordnungspolizei* serving in the *Waffen-SS* could wear the emblem of the *Ordnungspolizei*. Additional badges followed, like, for example, for former Hitler Youth leaders.

From the rank of *SS-Standartenführer*, officers in the SS Death's Head units wore a diamond with the Death's Head.

Officer in the judicial service.

OTHER INSIGNIA

The *edelweiss* for the caps worn by Waffen-SS mountain troops.

Left: The *edelweiss* for members of the SS mountain troops. It was worn on the right arm.

In units that did not have SS runes on their collar tabs, the *sigrunen* beneath the breast pocket showed, not only that the man was serving in the *Waffen-SS*, but also that he was a member of the SS. In the *SS-Polizei-Division* the badge was worn on green cloth—otherwise on black material.

August Schmidhuber (commander of *SS-Freiwilligen-Gebirgsjger-Regiment 14*, which was made up of ethnic Germans) with the *sigrunen* beneath his breast pocket.

On May 27, 1944, the Germans began recruiting fifteen- to twenty-year-old youths from the "still occupied" eastern lands to serve as so-called *SS-Helfer* (auxiliaries) or *SS-Zöglinge* (pupils). By September 20, 1944, 21,417 boys and girls were recruited from Russia, White Russia, the Ukraine, Lithuania, Latvia, and Estonia. As a rule, they were employed as flak auxiliaries in Germany. Later recruiting was concentrated in Hungary. If the *Waffen-SS* hoped to secure these youths as future replacements, it meant the complete abandonment of its earlier strict selection criteria.

Young Ukrainian *SS-Helfer* serving as *Luftwaffe* flak auxiliaries. Beneath the triangle with *sigrunen* (similar to the Hitler Youth district triangle) the boys are wearing an armband identifying their nationality.

As a rule, the badges were made simply by printing on thin fabric.

Waffen-SS recruiting poster for Russian youth (note the armband with the Andreas Cross): "Consider your future! Become an SS pupil."

Family portrait of an of an SS-NCO showing the *"Der Führer"* cuff title.

WAFFENFARBEN

Weiß	Infanterie
Hellblau	Versorgungstruppen
Kornblumenblau	Sanitäter
Schwarz	Pioniere
Dunkelgrau	Persönlicher Stab RF-SS
Hellgrau	Führer im Generalsrang
Hellbraun	Konzentrationslager
Hochrot	Artillerie
Karmesinrot	Veterinäre
Rosa	Panzer und Panzerjäger
Orangerot	Feldgendarmerie
Kupferbraun	Aufklärer
Hell-Lachsrosa	Wehrgeologen
Goldgelb	Kavallerie
Zitronengeld	Nachrichtentruppen
Hellgrün	Gebirgstruppen
Wiesengrün	Polizei-Schützen-Regimenter
Bordeauxrot	Nebelwerfer